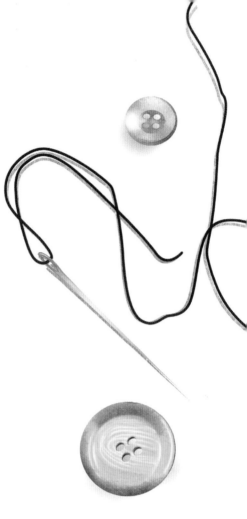

Dedicated to Annie,
Sophie, and Ralph
—D.B.

To Bernadette,
my guardian angel
—L.F.

little bee books

A division of Bonnier Publishing
853 Broadway, New York, New York 10003
Text copyright © 2017 by Deborah Blumenthal
Illustrations copyright © 2017 by Laura Freeman
All rights reserved, including the right of reproduction
in whole or in part in any form. LITTLE BEE BOOKS is a
trademark of Bonnier Publishing Group, and associated colophon is
a trademark of Bonnier Publishing Group.
Manufactured in China   LEO 0816
First Edition   10 9 8 7 6 5 4 3 2 1

Library of Congress Cataloging-in-Publication Data
Names: Blumenthal, Deborah, author. | Freeman, Laura (Illustrator), illustrator.
Title: Fancy Party Gowns : The Story of Fashion Designer Ann Cole Lowe /
by Deborah Blumenthal; illustrated by Laura Freeman.
Description: New York : Little Bee Books, 2017. | Audience: Ages 4-8. | Audience: K to grade 3.
Identifiers: LCCN 2015049772 | ISBN 9781499802399 (hardcover)
Subjects: LCSH: Lowe, Ann Cole, 1898-1981—Juvenile literature. | African American fashion designers—
Biography—Juvenile literature. | Women fashion designers—United States—Biography—
Juvenile literature. | Fashion design—United States—History—Juvenile literature.
Classification: LCC TT505.L69 B58 2017 | DDC 746.9/2092—dc23
LC record available at http://lccn.loc.gov/2015049772

ISBN 978-1-4998-0239-9

littlebeebooks.com
bonnierpublishing.com

FANCY PARTY GOWNS

THE STORY OF FASHION DESIGNER ANN COLE LOWE

by Deborah Blumenthal

little bee books

illustrated by Laura Freeman

When she was old enough
to thread a needle,
Ann Cole Lowe's momma
and grandma taught her
how to sew.

Wisps of cloth would fall
from their worktables like
confetti, and Ann would
scoop them up and turn
them into flowers as bright
as roses in the garden.

Ann's family came from
Alabama. Her great-grandma
had been a slave, so her
family knew about working
hard just to get by.

Ann also knew that doing what you love could set your spirit soaring.

So that's what she did, working near her momma in the family shop, making glorious dresses for women who went to fancy parties.

But when Ann was sixteen, death stole away her momma. There was no one to care for her anymore, and no one to make the dresses.

The Alabama governor's wife was waiting for her gowns.

Ann thought about what she could do, not what she couldn't change.

So she sat down and sewed the dresses herself. Then she stood up and ran the business.

In 1916 Ann got a job sewing dresses for a woman in Florida. A year later, the woman sent her to design school in New York. Ann was a good student and a fast learner.

But it was 1917, and Ann had to study in a separate classroom, all alone, because she was African American. And life wasn't fair.

Ann didn't make fine clothes to get rich or famous. She made them, she said, "To prove that a Negro can become a major dress designer."

Slowly, Ann got the recognition she deserved. In 1961 she was named "Official Couturiere" to honor her for the thirty-three Cinderella gowns she designed for a fancy ball in Omaha, Nebraska.

After so long, Ann stood up before fashion's biggest names, head held high, and they applauded her.

Ann Lowe

Hardly anyone knew something more important: the name of the woman who had created all those gowns, despite the odds.

Why?

Because Ann Cole Lowe was African American. And life wasn't fair.

That didn't stop Ann.

Famous women wore her gowns at big galas and on television.

"I like to hear about it," said Ann. "The oohs and aahs as they come into the ballroom."

Official Couturier

For Further Reading

"Ann Cole Lowe." The FMD. http://fashionmodeldirectory.com/designers/ann-cole-lowe/.

Alexander, Lois K. *Blacks in the History of Fashion*. New York: Harlem Institute of Fashion, 2008.

Bailey, Eric J. "African Americans in European American Mainstream Society's Fashion Industry: Early Years to the Present." *Black America, Body Beautiful: How the African American Image Is Changing Fashion, Fitness, and Other Industries*. Santa Barbara, CA: Praeger, 2008.

Lowe, Ann. Costume Institute at The Metropolitan Museum of Art. http://www.metmuseum.org/art/collection/search/83961.

Phelps, Timothy M. "Ann Lowe, 82, Designed Gowns for Exclusive Clientele in Society." *The New York Times*. March 1, 1981. http://www.nytimes.com/1981/03/01/obituaries/ann-lowe-82-designed-gowns-for-exclusive-clientele-in-society.html.

Powell, Margaret. "Ann Lowe and the Intriguing Couture Tradition of Ak-Sar-Ben." Nebraska History (Fall 2014): 134–143. http://www.nebraskahistory.org/publish/publicat/history/excerpts-3-14.htm.

Powell, Margaret. "The Life and Work of Ann Lowe: Rediscovering 'Society's Best Kept Secret.'" Master's diss., Smithsonian Associates and the Corcoran College of Art + Design, 2012.

Powell, Margaret. "The Remarkable Story of Ann Lowe: From Alabama to Madison Avenue." The National Archives: Pieces of History. March 28, 2013. http://blogs.archives.gov/prologue/?p=11922.

Reed Miller, Rosemary E. *Threads of Time: The Fabric of History*. 4th edition (eBook). T and S Press. October 5, 2011.

Werlin, Katy. "Ann Lowe's Early Career." The Fashion Historian. February 2014.

Wilson, Julee. "Ann Lowe: Black Fashion Designer Who Created Jacqueline Kennedy's Wedding Dress." Huffpost Black Voices. February 5, 2013. http://www.huffingtonpost.com/2013/02/05/ann-lowe-black-fashion-designer-jacqueline-kennedy-wedding-dress_n_2624316.html.

Author's Note

Ann Cole Lowe, born in 1898, was the first African American woman to become a designer of couture clothing. Between the 1920s and the 1960s, her one-of-a-kind designs were worn by various society women, such as the DuPonts, the Lodges, the Posts, and the Auchinclosses.

Ann is now best known for the ivory silk taffeta gown she designed for Jacqueline Bouvier's wedding to John F. Kennedy on September 12, 1953, at St. Mary's Church in Newport, Rhode Island. She is also known for designing the gown that Olivia de Havilland wore to the 1947 Academy Awards when she won the Best Actress award for her role in *To Each His Own*.

In her later years, Ann continued to design dresses for prominent women. She struggled financially though, and in 1960 was forced to close her salon in New York City. Ann continued her work until her retirement in 1972. She spent the last five years of her life living in Queens, New York.

While researchers of Ann's life will find inconsistencies in her biography, what is never in dispute is the extent of her talent.

Ann Cole Lowe died on February 25, 1981, at the age of 82.

The day of the wedding, all the world saw the future first lady of the United States, Jacqueline Bouvier Kennedy, in her magnificent gown, and her bridesmaids dressed in blush-pink silk faille.

She bought more fabric and trim, and hired others to help. She lost money instead of earning it.

In just eight days and eight nights, Ann and her team remade all the dresses.

But when Ann brought the gowns to the mansion in Newport, Rhode Island, where the wedding reception would take place, the butler who opened the door told her she'd have to use the back entrance that was meant for workers.

Ann said that if she had to enter through the back door, the bride and bridesmaids wouldn't be wearing her dresses for the wedding.

She entered through the front door.

Then just ten days
before the wedding,
Ann opened the door
to her workroom.

"NO!" she cried.

A pipe had burst.
Water gushed
everywhere, flooding
everything!

Ten of the sixteen
gowns were destroyed.

Ann thought about
what she could do,
not what she couldn't
change.

One day Ann got a special order. A lady in Washington, D.C., was marrying a senator. Seven years later, this man, John F. Kennedy, would become president of the United States.

Ann bought fifty yards of the finest ivory silk taffeta and the trimmings to go with it. For months she cut and sewed. The gown had a wide bouffant skirt with pleated bands and tiny wax flowers.

Ann also made all the dresses for the wedding party.

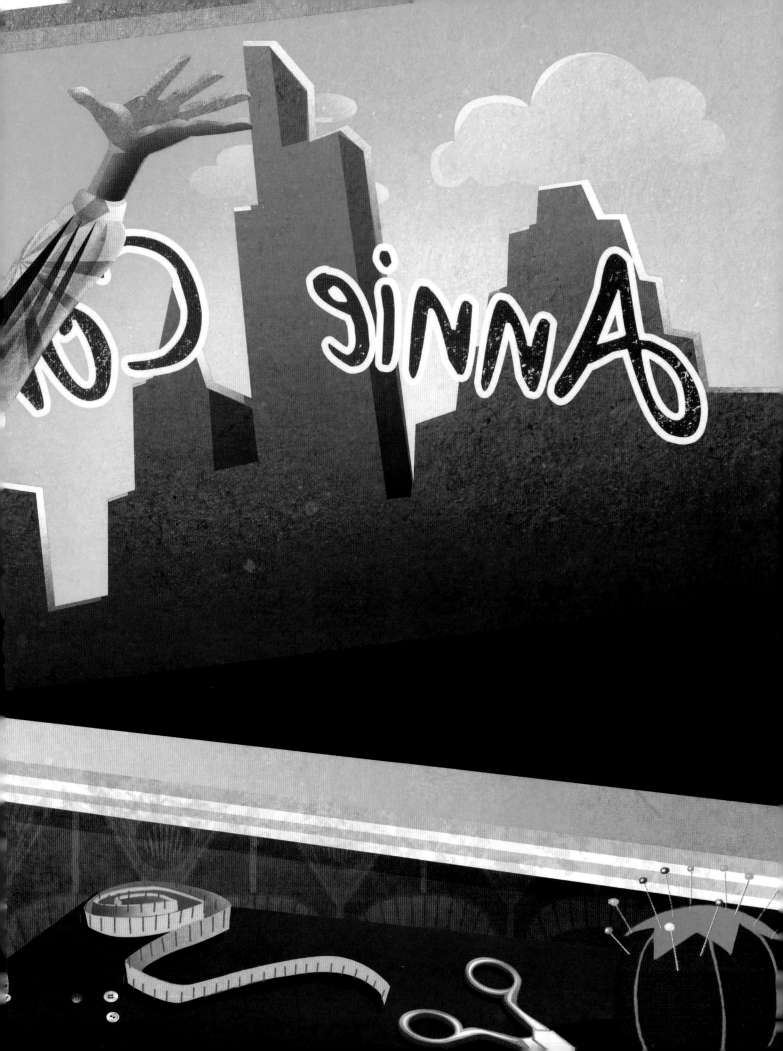

"I feel so happy when I am making clothes that I could just jump up and down with joy," she said.

Finally, Ann saved enough money to open a salon of her own in Manhattan. She had big bills to pay, and sometimes not enough money to pay them.

That didn't stop her. When Ann saw obstacles, she thought about what she could do, not what she couldn't change.

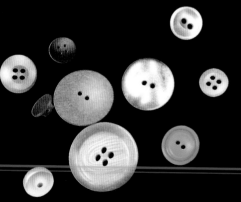

That didn't stop Ann.

She kept on making extravagant gowns, and year after year more and more women wanted to wear them.

Elegant dresses.

Party gowns.

No two alike.